"Gerson's country, a landscape haunted by echoes of the past, by wind and absence, is brought to vivid life by the stark, lean poems of *Once Planed Straight*. His work captures a time and place that many might overlook or dismiss, whether of small-town diners, rock bluffs, or abandoned barns. With authenticity as well as poignant humanity, Steve Gerson observes moments of quiet, ghostly beauty, "a post oak corral/fencing memories" or "the muffled breeze of a distant hummingbird's wings" on a slight promontory of prairie grass."

-Tom Reynolds, author of *Ghost Town Almanac* and *Home Field,* Woodley Press.

"*Once Planed Straight* reminds us that the heart and soul of the American dream thrived not so long ago in the small towns and farms fast disappearing from our Midwest landscape. These evocative poems give us a nuanced and often heartbreaking glimpse into what we've left behind."

-Edie Cottrell Kreisler, Professor Emeritus, Merritt College

"Steve Gerson's poetry collection locates readers in a place of "absence" and "silence" and then gifts them the moon and "purple prairie clover." The poetry in this book contains the subtlety and complexity of a sunset on the Flint Hills. Gerson has divided the book into sections, rooting readers in "place" first and leading them to "love" in the end. He reminds us that when we lose our aspirations and our sense of place, there is still something left to love. *Once Planed Straight* woos readers with evocative sensory images and alliteration. In the end, readers are left with the sense that Gerson has "gifted [them] the morning mist."

>   -Beth Gulley, author of *I Am Your Fish Drowning In Air: Love Poems*, *The Sticky Note Alphabet*, and *$!*# Hole Countries: A Find and Replace Meditation*.

"Striking images of nature, coupled with the haunting remnants of old grain silos, dilapidated barns, and wire fences, provide readers a notion of a pioneer spirit long departed, even as the land continues to evolve unabated."

>   -Jim McWard, Ph.D., Professor, English, Johnson County Community College

Once Planed Straight

Poems of the Prairies
Steve Gerson

Spartan Pres
Kansas City, MO
spartanpress.com

Spartan Press

Copyright © Steve Gerson, 2021
First Edition: 1 3 5 7 9 10 8 6 4 2
ISBN: 978-1-952411-83-0
LCCN: 2021950388

Cover photo:© COPYRIGHT 2016 Mark Feiden
All rights reserved. No part of this publication may be
reproduced or transmitted in any form or by any means,
electronic or mechanical, including photocopying,
recording or by info retrieval system, without prior
written permission from the author.

Acknowledgements

The following poems first appeared either in print or online:

"Reflection under Yellow Sky:" *The Write Launch.*
"When fields bloom dust:" *Underwood Press.*
"Still Life, Spring:" *The Decadent Review.*
"Missing:" *Variant Literature Journal.*
"Morning Mist:" *Underwood Press.*
"Edge:" *Ink & Voices.*
"Abandoned:" *Coffin Bell Journal.*
"Reclaimed:" *Abstract.*
"Empty:" *Panoplyzine.*
"Once Planed Straight:" *Panoplyzine.*
"Time spinning shadows:" *Underwood Press.*
"Played Out:" *The Dillydoun Review.*
"Path:" *Panoplyzine.*
"Moored:" *The Hungry Chimera.*
"Calendar Pages Yellowing:" *Panoplyzine.*
"Widow's Window:" *Route 7 Review.*
"First it giveth:" *In Parentheses.*
"Abuela en Las Estrellas:" *The Antonym.*
"woman suffocating under skyless clouds." *Variant Literature Journal.*
"You next to me:" *Route 7 Review.*
"After 10 days roughnecking Oklahoma oilfields:" *Panoplyzine.*
"Her Dress Once Pink:" *Abstract.*
"Modern love:" *Montana Mouthful.*
"Barbed:" *South Florida Poetry Journal.*

Table of Contents

Overview

Place

Synapse / 1

The curvature of the earth / 2

Flatlands / 3

Reflection under Yellow Sky / 4

Unfettered / 5

Absence / 6

Prairie / 7

Pastoral / 8

When fields bloom dust / 9

Still Life, Spring / 10

Confluence: lines on Roxy Paine's "Ferment" / 12

Missing / 13

Shelter

Sentinel / 17

Morning Mist / 18

edge / 19

Abandoned / 20

Reclaimed / 21

Empty / 22

Once Planed Straight / 23

Aspiration

Time spinning shadows / 27

Played Out / 28

Path / 30

Moored / 31

Diablo / 32

Calendar Pages Yellowing / 34

Widow's Window / 35

First it giveth / 36

Abuela en Las Estrellas / 37

Triptych—Coffin Bell, Rung, No Answer / 40

Love

A Gentle Rise / 45

Mountaintop aspiring / 46

Reflecting / 47

woman suffocating under skyless clouds / 49

You next to me / 50

After 10 days roughnecking Oklahoma oilfields / 51

Her dress once pink / 52

Modern love / 53

Barbed / 54

Overview

There was a time when the plains and prairies were aspirational. Early settlers, hemmed in on the East coast by the Atlantic, looked beyond the Appalachians toward the setting sun, toward the wolf's howl . . . and wondered.

Then these intrepid pioneers, in the words of Mark Twain, lit out "for the Territory ahead of the rest."

Some continued beyond the great inland ocean between Missouri's western fringe of central hardwoods and Colorado's mountain crests. Some forged rivers and climbed the Rockies to discover California and Oregon.

Others settled along the Missouri River, the Kaw, the Platte, and the Cheyenne. In these great plains, they built small towns and small farms and Midwestern lifestyles. They fenced in land, corralled livestock, built barns and silos and schools and businesses and churches.

In time, they were met with wind, drought, locusts, tornadoes, blight, barbed wire, and eventually airplanes flying overhead from coast to coast. After generations, children migrated from the small towns and settled in larger cities. And the small towns shrank in population, the barns sank into the fields, and crops moldered.

This is not a chapbook of nostalgia. The poems in this collection focus on what was once planed straight in pristine planks but what bent askew in time.

To Sharon, my inspiration

> I knocked and waited
> For a life to come
> Did you wait too
> I heard your steps
> Did you hear my breath intake
> Did your hands anticipate
> That our hands would join
> You on one side of a door
> We at the threshold

Once Planed Straight

Place

Ashen prairie fire
Silhouetting a lone tree—
Emptiness scorches.

Synapse

From Ogallah to Neligh, Owanka to Medora
the great American Pleistocene sea
drained to dry chalk rock flint limestone shale
submerging cretaceous fish and toothed birds
unearthing fossils covered by prairieland
covering sedimentary oil gas and gold
reigned by Arapaho Lakota Ojibwa and Crow
passed through these plains Santa Fe
Oregon and California trails
sailed over this land by Lewis and Clark
pioneers and settlers leaping the continental
synapse between Missouri's western fringe
of central hardwoods and Colorado's mountain crests
the tallgrass plains America's connective tissue

The curvature of the earth

On a grey morning,
The horizon closes
When sky clouds meet ground fog,
Transboundary haze limiting vistas.

Desiccated trees belt
Fields of just cropped corn,
Stalks ragged on rutted ground
In late Fall, early Winter.

Birds flown like migrating leaves,
The land muffled, snow silenced,
The compressed world waits weary
For our axis to tilt sunward.

With Spring, mist dissipates to lighten darkness.
Fields open to the curvature of the earth.

Flatlands

the flatlands of absence where sound is silent
where migrant tallgrass and wayward cottonwood
compete with bluestem and dry wind

empty limitlessness when wisp of line between plain
    and sky
snakes circumnavigating surrounding with distant
    sibilance
the hum of expectation the moan of despair

look behind to see nothing look forward and see no more

Reflection under Yellow Sky

Sitting at a counter in the stoplight diner,
I stared out the window, you staring back at me.
The traffic had travelled down FM 202,
Leaving the road dusty, chaff-filled
After the thresher had fed.
Only you kept me company.
In the glass, streaked by age and dirt,
Each line an alluvial fissure, life washing out to sea,
You blurred me in the reflected glare.
The coffee-steamed distortion,
One eye slightly drooped, lowering my sights,
That mouth a gill slit, air gulping the yellow sky,
Hair sprouting like winter wheat shocks missed in the corner field,
I took a sip of my stewed coffee, reflecting.

Unfettered

Not the claustrophobia of California
redwoods suffocating seedlings
moldering in deferred dreams or
New York's skeletal steel streets
walled eyes averted manholes

But Black Hill bluffs and
mesas hillocks and crag slate
embracing bison and bighorn
towering over skittish squirrels
and guarding masked shrew

Slanted shafts of light through
slats of cloud casting shadows
on wind wending through ravines
hush roiling into roar and in the
distance only distance unfettered

Absence

within the voiceless void
of black evening sky
desolate as prairie vistas
in lifeless winter hibernating
stars sing songs of grassland silence
shuddering as pronghorns flee predator
wolves who stalk the silence resounding
as sound their absence obscuring
what isn't to deceive appearance

Prairie

any hillock from overlooks expanse
distance empty line between land
and eternity sky nothingness turn
around turn around to same all air

sound the rush of pulse within but
on ground to step a grouse on buffalo
grass tanned yellow gray by winds
whistling from behind the moon toward

settling through rifts in low hills rock
stream scribed cow tongued and
within the null a purple prairie clover
peeks above flint hardscrabble like want

Pastoral

it's the way the wind bends the stalks supplicant
like a nun's prayer yes, the world is viral twisted

tweets in rootless trees pundit noises insta intrusions
social media drilling misinformation into earbuds worming

into glazed eyes but past the roil of fury out my window
past pine pole corrals and the mare beaten earth of a paddock

toward baled hay and deer path squirrel twitch and geese flight
the sky softens sound thought steeps like porch tea

and the wind not a wheedle through hoarse coarse TV screed
wends between the pin oak and sycamore cottonwood and elm

in my prairie and shivers the stilled leaves pirouetting as chimes
my boot heeled steps trod mist morning cracking wheat shards

and corn husks yellow as the moon setting and the world
   weary burrows
beneath where finch wren and thrush whistle into the sibilance
   of silence

When fields bloom dust

the town once had a picture show with balcony
and jujubes and news shorts about some war
and cartoons where animals met violent ends

when life was black and white it maybe cost a dime
Realto or Roxy Princess or Palace can't remember
the name with velvet curtains and uniformed ushers

the marquee paint faded in yellow bruises and paper
promos blotched like mottled skin beneath cataract
glass the show moved out when the drugstore closed

when the doctor died and the Farmers Insurance Co.
repossessed our farm and sold our tractor for a quarter
on the dollar I watched them haul away the dining room

table and grandma's chester drawers the two mules that
pulled our cart gone too with two cows and a calf
they left Dad's neckerchief once red now pale as

platelets our fields bloom dust from withered vines
and dust covers the town square a stray cat's mew
whines like a nail hammered into coffin pine

Still Life, Spring

As Spring. Into the plains, south of Abilene, north of Wichita,
Kansas prairieland, where May's rain streams like wreathed
smiles and lark song flies in dappled skies, tallgrass wends

with prairie smoke, sweetbriar, clover, and blazing star.
 Bluestem
flowers white against the setting sun, exhaling in a throe,
 sizzling the
memory of winter, burrowing in fallow ground, dirt deep
 in milo fields.

Sheaves of wheat grow sun yellow amid red barns, their
 doors open
in heaving sighs. Dry seedlings sprout. Corn greens on
 husks, their amber
tassels trembling in Springtime's freshening breezes. Amid
 the whistle

of swallow and sparrow, kingbird and warbler, the chug of
 tractors
scythe to plough furrows in pied daisies, uplifting the land
 from
its winter knell. The sky is blue and shaded with powder
 whiffs,

cloud shadows lazy upon the curvature of the earth. Hawks
 wheel,

their chests white against the cirrus striations, white as
   hope from a once dark
world. I've become the plains, their hillocks a maze of
   marvel, charmed

by the distance of distance. I've become Spring, as wind weaves
through a lone cottonwood's quiet leaves, the nearest sounds
a windmill's whisper, a cow's lowing call to romance.

Confluence: lines on Roxy Paine's "Ferment"

iron roots thrusting down toward firmament,
sunk deep into prairie sod to eek strength from bedrock
and turbulent ferment of uplifted river bottom topsoil
at the confluence of a city's foundation, where the Missouri
meets the Kansas,

branches soaring toward aspiration, each arm
a metallic current electrifying neuron dendrites roiling
like the rivers, each arm gleaming of sky images
and a diverse populace reflecting prismatic, melding like
molten chrome, like jazz improvisation,

trunk stout, bulbous nerve cells and axons of connectivity
where a city's energy grows from a hub of rich loam radiating
like railway lines, from a frontier spirit sprinting as through
high-speed spectrums, an artful confluence of quicksilver
   science,
the tree surges.

Missing

Three black crows perch
on the school's wire fence,
scoping the fields beyond for prey
where the fields bleed into the diminishing
horizon. Above, a harrier hawk wheels
on the gray March clouds.
A windmill nearby turns slowly,
one blade missing,
the other blades rusted like
blooming spores.
Its metal lurches,
struggling to find a breeze
in the drought-ridden sky and whirs
like locusts gnawing on dry stalks.
The school yard is empty,
the playground equipment swinging
in the dead air, the metal clanging
against the sound of a distant siren's knell.

Shelter

Near the fields, the barn
Sat still, its post oak corral
Fencing memories.

Sentinel

The silo stands sentinel,
Superego to the barn's id,
The barn doors flung wide,

Inviting children's summer play,
Swinging from the hay hoist,
October called dances

With stolen embraces,
A March romantic interlude in the loft
Under a bat's roost, an owl's screech,

The barn's peaked ridges angular
Rebelling against the flatland prairie,
Reddened with passion,

At odds with tasseled corn and tawny wheat,
Lights ablaze from the barn's casements,
Enticing.

The silo is battened,
At right angles to the horizon,
Rising righteously to protect last year's crop

Airlessly encased.
Looking windowless down upon the land,
Impervious, mortared in rigid alignment,

The silo's bricks still beside the breathing barn's wooden slats.

Morning Mist

On weekdays, always hot in the southern South,
I'd smell the coffee before even awake,
even through the humidity, as present as the family dog,
my dreams made brown from the blackening dregs,
then hear him gently banging cupboards,
trying to still the family's sleep.
He'd ease the door and touch my foot, saying,
"Come on bud, the day's awake,"
and I'd rise to meet him, me, alone, the others abed,
my feet on the warmth of the cedar floors, his warmth
having walked ahead. There on the table he'd set two mugs,
his coffee as black as the fields we worked, mine, with milk,
the color of November dawn. He'd chow down on bacon and
eggs, dabbing ketchup on each bite. I tried to match him mouth
for mouth, falling short by an egg or two. "Can you feel the
change, bud? Saw them geese flyin' farther south and the wooly
worms out, too. Cold is coming, but there's time to plant some
turnips or collards for mom to can when winter hits. So eat up,
boy, we got work to do," tousling my hair of winter wheat.
Then off we'd trudge. I jumped to match each step he strode,
I the circle from the stone he'd thrown. Once in the field, he
took the heavy load, the spade and rake while I sprinkled seeds
on the rows he hoed. I wasn't needed to work the land.
He gifted me the morning mist.

edge

trailing a smog
as thick as a swarm
of mosquitos
leave behind the city
to find the edge
where exhaustion
thins
leap the synapse
the border between pavement and gravel
the ordered alignment
of right angled boards
hard lines that curb
seek the deflection of
rough barked forest
and lake shapes
where nothing is squared

Abandoned

stepping from the tree break
the rabbit slung over my shoulder
head down tethered by withered sinew
one red pearl adorning its winter white ruff

a harvested cornfield before me barren to disuse
now a shard of bones cracking underfoot
the abandoned house beyond it
paint mottled like age spots sun singed

I studied the shack
a skull with vortex windows darkened
the door a splintered maw
wooden slats jagged as gnawed teeth

a cold wind moaned as through a bone flute
scattering the shed's memories across the broken field

Reclaimed

The barn thrived for three generations,
barn doors flung wide hosting children on thrown hay,
October called dances with stolen embraces beneath roof
    pitch and wood fail,
the breeze joyous in the wheat, its golden hue reflecting
    on the barn's whitewash.

In '08 a plank or two loosened,
field mice and copperheads sibilant in the silo hold,
    farm loans a fault
on the tectonic plate, a crow's shriek, but murmured
    urgings within the soil,
whispers swirling within the windbreak, the wood's
    memory, upwelled.

When trade tariffs reaped the wheat,
unbaled, strewn on the ground like locust husks blackened,
crops moldering in suffocated dreams,
the breeze stilled, succumbing to cicada sirens.

The barn stooped, wizened beams arthritic,
reclaimed by kudzu coiling.

Empty

The bow-backed barn shuttered tight
Slumps into the barren field
Drawn down by gravitational pull
Of generations escaping, the past
Abandoned like winter cut wheat remnants
Moldering in the hayless loft.
The loft, backlit by slanted light
Prying through planks once planed,
Now warps with disregarding drafts,
Silence only marred by creaks,
Voiceless where children's voices had sung,
Airless where lovers had breathlessly breathed,
Emptied of anticipation,
Empty but for wavering motes.

Once Planed Straight

The barn leaning leeward,
Buffeted by the plain's prevalent winds,
Recollects harvests cast away.
Boards, missing in halves and thirds,
Moan like wind through marrowless bones,
Barely enough batten standing sturdy to right what remains.
Fringing the boarded base, broken wheat shafts
Angle unnaturally, no longer seeking the sun
But wearied by wind and lost purpose.
Offering a slanted view within and without,
A wicket gate placed in the barn door
Hangs on missing bolts, rusted Kodachrome amber.
The barn's truth, once planed straight,
Now looks instead askew.

Aspiration

Out the window, past
the poplar windbreak, open
fields stretch endlessly.

Time spinning shadows

I can't grow wind he said to her
as he stood in the field once black
from prairie fire once rich in topsoil
now the shade of cadavers just dead

Gone where life had grown his family
gone too parents and grandparents and
even prior generations like seasons
remembering rows of crop and hands

Turning now what turns are the rows of
windmills that loom and lurch metal
beasts that whir like locusts eating
not breezes singing within the stalks

The bank that repossessed his legacy
withered on spent vines suggested wind
sell air they said your day's done let the
windmills work the land you failed

What spins are my hands wringing
calloused knuckles grinding skin
once tanned and creased and split
a map for my children to follow

That map useless as dry parchment cracked
what can I do he wailed with idle hands
sit and watch time spin shadows on our
land now the bank's I can't grow wind

Played Out

When the farm played out,
trees growing in the silos

untended where mice chewed
corn dust, where the rocker

on the house's paint-pealed porch
screamed ghostly on wormed wood,

wind whistling through broken slats,
he left, replacing his lame nag,

swaybacked and crop weary,
with a job in the city driving a truck.

He still wore his Stetson Llano
cowboy hat, the straw stained

the color of time, dried and storm blown,
his dungarees patched with worn dreams,

his work boots gnarled as hands torn
on barbed wire. He still drove the truck

like a horse at walk gait, broken from a day
of pulling plow, throat latch choked,

hame heavy, backstrap girded as tight
as a candle snuffed without a wish made,

and he peered into his rearview mirror
fearing the next blue norther looming.

Path

Wheel ruts,
scythe rows
in a soybean field
point pole star north
intersecting at right angles
with the rim of the earth.
From his front porch,
mottled hands mapping the land,
grasping the pied railing,
the sun rising in his periphery,
he surveys this path plumbed true,
mist on the pasture.
But east to west shadows parallel I-80,
roughhewn flatland prairie
becoming straight-line Pacific.
In the distance,
the bus's dust plumes,
nearing.

Moored

The canoe moored to a ten-foot dock,
Weathered, warped, wearied,
Rides high on a low waterline,
Snow melt distant.

Two worm-holed paddles
Crisscross on the hull ribs,
One cracked like a Mississippi delta,
Alluvial fissures running through the blade.

Rusted marsh reeds, land born,
Encroach the bay and crowd the canoe,
Suffocating with silt and leaf scorch.
The reeds obscure the horizon.

The setting sun, weaving its rays
Through the reeds, entices,
Plains rivers burbling.
The canoe dreams of voyaging.

Diablo

1872, a war done, the men headed west,
their lands back home now growing bone shards.
They followed the sun and fled shadows.
The Piedmont they left was shrouded in loblolly pitch,

where pine straw hid the land and wind wove
breathless between choked branches.
The open plains ahead rolled treeless with promise.
Caleb busted broncs near the South Platte

while yahoos ringing the found-wood corrals
hurrahed, waving their kepis, blue and gray.
"You ride that sonabitch, Caleb boy.
Grab 'im by his ears if ya' have to.

Let 'im know you the boss man," shouted a cowpoke
wearing a ragged tartan plaid shirt tucked into his denims,
patched with baling hay and tar,
a cigar dangling from his spit-spewing mouth.

Caleb sat high on the withers, back on the haunch
of a stallion dubbed Diablo, black as an eclipse,
the horse spinning like a dust devil in a dry wind.
His hand in the mane, Caleb hung on, like he did

in Wilmington at Cape Fear. "I beat the war before it beat me.
I'll beat this damn plug too," despite the hooves sharp as
sabers Diablo's teeth nipping at his chaps. Horse and man
rose in a whirl, Diablo's back twisting tornadic

toward roiling skies, Caleb spinning to counter the torque,
then down they landed like God's fist pounding
the earth on the third day of creation.
Rather than rise in a new fevered buck,

Diablo fell on its flank to dislodge the rider.
And Caleb was pinned beneath lathered flesh,
a ton of horse, muscle and sinew.
The hurrahing stopped like the crack of a bone.

As the devil stood and cowboy stayed prone,
the west won what war could not kill.

Calendar Pages Yellowing

I creaked up the back porch stairs
and opened and slammed the torn screen door
and swatted away a buzzing fly
the memory of a past day gone

with picnics near the fallow fields
the whining wail of harmonicas
and hand churned ice cream cherry or peach
the pits and stones breaking teeth

and walked into the kitchen dark
from blinds drawn and eyes shut
to recent sickness and palsied hands.
Mom stood at the farmhouse sink

calendar pages yellowing
a glass of milky water filled
and tilting up to take a swig
her other hand holding pills

too many for a daily dose.
Out the window barely cracked
I caught a glimpse of tractors stilled
leafless trees and murderous crows.

Widow's Window

The evening light, more gray than dusk yellow,
filtering through cracked windowpanes as dust,
cast shadows on her threadbare dress like faded
bones. She rested one hand on the chilled sill,
the other on her brow bowed low. Outside,
her farm's fallow fields dimmed in the November
nightfall, the air breathless as a shuttered cellar,
canned goods lined cobwebbed like tombstones.
The route from 96, Bismarck to Mandan,
passed without a glance, she a postscript, a postcard
never delivered. A mongrel cur, one ear clipped
like a bus ticket collected, trudged down the weed-strewn
road wending toward her home and wandered off like
a memory. Looking up, she saw the night's last light fade.

First it giveth

Dressed in muddied hip waders, an orange U-Haul
gimme hat, a T-shirt holey as Easter Sunday, Silas
paddled his shallow draft over the bayou, hunting a
croc, cottonmouth, or cat, whatever.

The day gray with humidity, the sky green with the threat
of squalls, Silas heard the swamp's despair. Frogs groaned
loss; mosquitoes hissed like hope seeping through low-ceiling
cloud cover. "I need me a catch,"

Silas wheezed, sucking on a Pall Mall. "Need it bad. My God.
My God, what you want?" Then he felt a tug, the twinge of a
slow pulse. His line quivered. A droplet of brackish water
trilled from the nylon cord, the line

ascending against the swamp's dominion where mangroves
and mud protect their own. The line tightened until the mossy
back of a snapping turtle surfaced, one red eye glaring.
Rain started, a drop, two, then a gully washer, clouds suffocating

the swamp, air turning black as a tilled field, the bayou churning.
Silas' canoe twisted in an eddy, snagging his line on a stump,
the cord limp in his hand. His snapper sunk beneath the murk

like repossessed credit. "Damn," he muttered. Sitting in the
barren belly of his rig, Silas thought about his family's hunger,
migration of waterfowl, inevitably of tides, travel of planets
over the bayou, and baited a new hook.

Abuela en Las Estrellas

"Ven aqui, nieto mio," my grandfather said as he pushed back
his worn Stetson, dust colored and weathered like the rutted

road leading to our small farm 10 miles south of Taos.
The night lights from Santa Fe were a haze on the horizon,

past mesquite and sagebrush. Above us the sky was midnight dark.
He placed his arm around my shoulder, caressing, and pointed

skyward with a gnarled finger. "Mi padre said that Dios created
stars by holding fire in his hand and blowing springtime gusts,

so embers sparkled el cielo. The embers light our life's path."
Then tracing routes from one star to another, my abuelo said,

"See that star in the southeast? It's Cetus, the sea monster.
That's where our family began, when mi hermano Roberto and I

left the coast of Veracruz con six pesos and a tattered bag of cornmeal
sealed in plantain peels. We trod like pack animals through Mexico,

through the Chihuahuan Desert, through saguaro thorns and dry gulch
bones to find Estados Unidos, crossing the border at El Paso, knee deep

in the Rio. Follow my finger, mijo" as he inched up toward Aries
then Perseus, mapping the route as if the sky was parchment
and he the

calligrapher. "Tu madre, her family came to Taos from
picking apples in
Kansas City, cutting hay near Wichita, then working the
meat plants in Dodge City,

migrating southwest with the seasons." He touched Lacerta
the lizard star and
tracked his hand downward toward Cassiopeia to Aunga,
"as if they rode

the charioteer's celestial wagon. What drew us like gravity,
like solar
magnetism was your abuela, mi encantadora. She was the
Estrella del Norte,

the north star on my journey, already living in Taos, waiting
for her life to
flare, my life to flame," he said, his hand gripping my shoulder,
his breath

misting in the night's cooling air. "There," he said, leaning his
head against mine,
stretching his hand higher, so that his frayed chambray work
shirt fell below his

knobbed wrist, his voice quavering like the heaven's music,
"there she is, our abuelita,

glowing in the night, the center of our universe, we her swirling constellation.

Her luz illumines our retinas.
We breathe her starlight."

Triptych—Coffin Bell, Rung, No Answer

1.
He stood by the store's front door,
his arms crossed, shoulders hunched,
staring at the floor.

The tiny bell above the door,
asthmatic, breathed
nothing.

A hairline crack in the front window
refracted spider webs
on the yellowing linoleum.

Outside, the marquee's missing letters advertised,
"B y fiv ha f pric , get   nex f ve FREE!"
a come-on guaranteeing

2.

failure. His shop losing money, nibbling at
bankruptcy like field mice chewing wallboard,
his store, near the outskirts of town,

close to where the pavement ended
and streets became gravel roads,
was empty,

at the corner of next and was,
the intersection of will and gone,
a one-stoplight crossroad.

His shop had been empty since the three-story
superstore moved in up the highway,
last exit.

3.

That bookstore offered baristas, scones, graphic
novels, t-shirts of Sylvia Plath and Ernest Hemingway,
and a drive through.

Now once-valued readers passed his shop
like air hissing from a flattening tire.
He raised his gaze

with the heft of a horsehead
on a pumpjack drilling dry wells,
the bit caught on sunken bones

and breathed in the hollow air. His empty store
smelled of dust-jacketed books disused,
the hushed voices of shelved writers.

Love

Through the door, the bed,
Once with two warm furrows, is
Wintering, fallow.

A Gentle Rise

On a promontory,
Only a gentle rise,
360º views of prairie and plain
The world revolves

With hailstorms in the Midwest,
Carriers sailing toward Korea,
Wall Street traders flashing semaphores,
Babies being born in Brazilian favelas,
Polar bears leaping ice floes,
Chefs touting quinoa,
House invasions in Paris,
Some Kardashian promoting some self-interest,

A bully, a beauty,
A poet, a publisher,
An artist, an audience,
A nuclear reactor, a rainbow.

You and I stand on the slight mound,
Touching or not,
Within reach of each other,
The world's noise on our prairie plateau
The muffled breeze of a distant hummingbird's wings.

Mountaintop aspiring

From prairie plain through foothills mild,
Mountaintop aspiring,
Running rocky with ravines and snow melt,
Rises upward upward
Toward a peak where winds refresh with air like breath.

Mountainhigh, in a clearing,
A nine-tree grove of aspens stands.
Two tall trees center rise,
As four ring the borderline,
Encircling three saplings small.

Beneath the soil clonal roots
Emerge from a mother's boll,
To strengthen through a shared resolve,
Family varied as branch and bark,
Variegated leaf and seed.

The grove crowns the crest
With arms spread wide
Embracing joyous inhaling visions
Of horizons backlit by an eastern sun
Escalating, a glorious dawn.

Reflecting

Dad made two sandwiches each,
bread, butter, sugar, wrapped
in wax paper, secured by yellow and red

toothpicks, packed in his knapsack,
near the thermos of hot coffee
that when opened spumed mist

into the January morning chill,
mist like our breaths, mist like that
rising from the gray-blue lake

reflecting the winter clouds.
Duck season. Kansas plains.
We huddled behind the cattails

and peered through our blind slats,
Dad working the duck call "blather blather."
"I'm cold, Dad," I said shivering.

Dad glanced at me, winking,
laid down his double aught, scooted over,
and placed his right arm around

my shoulder, his field coat
the color of my auburn hair,
my hair reflecting his sandy beard.

"Cuddle up sis." We only saw
four ducks that morning,
a drake, a hen, and their brood,

lazing on the ice-crusted water, reflecting
the dawn sky. "No shootin' today hon.
We're gonna leave that little family alone.

Let's eat them sandwiches and enjoy the lake."
I hugged him closer, I recall, now
winters later, thumbing through

a Kodak-tinged photo album, remembering
how we watched the sun dissipate the winter
chill, reflecting our warmth.

woman suffocating under skyless clouds

bovine in her way
dressed uniformly in muddied russet

glazed cow-stare straight
like vacant windows in farm outbuildings
black as eyeless sockets

she endures self-stockaded
as if muzzling stray blades
of grass on barren browned fields
downward gazing under leafless trees
every day a late fall

not always so numbed
she once effervesced
I recall her eyes uplifted yearning
after passing planes flying elsewhere
contrails etching sun-streaked paths

but life intervened siloing her
a romance denied her moans lowing
a career curtailed cowering
friendships family all plowed under
climate changes in her soul

till tariffed by slights her sights low
she ruminates suffocating under skyless clouds

You next to me

my face a dry well
palms etched as wormed wood

I'm obscured by a windbreak
of barbed locust circling

our farm like carrion crow
outside my kitchen window

black curtained by oilskin
and smoke-tinged flyspeck

our fields of frozen shards
cut wheat where your downed

pheasant redden the snow
moon smudged by night fog

smothering the land breathing
shallow wind wailing whistles

through broken teeth you next
to me in bed a meteor crashing

After 10 days roughnecking Oklahoma oilfields

he's driving toward me
not as fast as electricity
sizzles through bowing lines
or stanchions erect ringing
the curvature of the earth
but with the same hum
of high-voltage energy
discharging corroded rust
on sun riven roads
his approach anticipatory
bringing either heat that touches
me like his grasp on a longneck bottle
fingers thrumming or the rumble
of distant clouds thundering
on the horizon to crush me
like a beer can tossed carelessly
in his pickup's dusty bed

Her Dress Once Pink

A prairie hawk on a snow-mounded fence
a wake of buzzards on the gray wind
shocks of yellow winter wheat on the periphery
the field bleeding into the horizon

I   can't   go   on
she said surrounded by absence
the air a hole consuming sound
our nearest neighbors only dust plumes conversing

You work the land
feel the soil warm your soles
blacken your fingers coiling around roots
to coax growth out of riven sod

The breeze swirls around you in embrace
she said I'm in your grandpa's house
built by prior generations
of seekers who left leaving motes

Wearing a dress once pink
now the color of leeched corpuscles
my palms etched like drought-baked clay
I'm   growing   emptiness

The jet flying 50,000 feet above
our farmstead she said sees
the curvature of the earth obscured by the windbreak
casting shadows through my window

Modern love

I'm driving the pickup, once heart red
now fading to muddied oxblood
like our dun cows and as haggard,

the bed beat up from my careless throwing
of things like fenceposts and accusations,
to the end of our road, and I'm looking back

at the farm through the rearview, late November sky
the color of excuses weary in the leafless trees,
our fields barren so even the sheep can barely muzzle

blades, our doublewide listing on its tired foundation,
a rigged tarp flapping at our bedroom, failure
to discourage the Fall, all the windows in the house

and outbuildings as black as a murder of crows, as
 unharvested
promises blackening on the vine, and those heifers a
 Greek chorus
their all-seeing eyes cow-staring a rebuke.

I've stopped the truck. The only sounds are the whine
of the engine once hot now cold and the dissipating
moan of your plane overhead flying elsewhere.

Barbed

The barbed wire strung between the pine poles sang
like a guillotine in the November gusts. Cattle lowing,
plaintive, huddled near the fallen post oak, felled

by lightning strikes, the night air still sizzling with
ashen embers and despair. I saw slivers of the moon
behind a black cloud in the black sky, the pale light

leaching like spoiled milk. "Not now, Claire," he said,
his words pulled like a rusted nail from a dry board.
I thumbed a loose thread around the tear in my worn dress.

"When?" I asked, the cattle still calling in the fields amid
more lightning flashes. He turned and stared. "Not ever,"
as the backdoor slammed, its wire screen shuddering.

Dr. Steven M. Gerson (PhD, Texas Tech) retired from Johnson County Community College in 2016 after 38 years of teaching. He then taught at the University of Kansas Medical Center's Health Information Management Program from 2017-2021.

He is the 2003-2004 Kansas Professor of the Year, chosen by the Carnegie Foundation. Steve is also a Society for Technical Communication Fellow, the highest award given by the society for outstanding contributions to the discipline; a recipient of the 2016 Jay R. Gould Award for Excellence in Teaching Technical Communication, an international award for mentorship, scholarship, and innovation and creativity in teaching; and the Council for Programs in Technical and Scientific Communication's 2021 Distinguished Service Award winner. He is the co-author, along with his wife Sharon Gerson, of *Technical Communication: Process and Product* (Prentice Hall, 9th edition), *Writing That Works: A Teacher's Guide to Technical Writing* (2nd edition, Kansas State Dept. of Education), *Workplace Communication: Process and Product* (Prentice Hall, 1st edition), and *Workplace Writing: Planning, Packaging, and Perfecting* (Prentice Hall, 1st edition).

Steve has published over 100 poems in *Panoplyzine* (winning an Editor's Choice award), *Hungry Chimera, Toe Good, Write Launch, Route 7, Duck Lake, Coffin Bell, Poets Reading the News, Crack the Spine, White Wall Review, Variant, Abstract, Montana Mouthful, Decadent Review, Indolent, Rainbow Poems, Snapdragon, Underwood Press, Wingless Dreamer, Gemini Ink, Dillydoun Review, Elevation Review, Poet's Choice, Lucky Jefferson, Novus Literary, In Parentheses, South Florida Poetry Journal, 86 Logic, Two Timbers,* and *Constellations*. He's proud to have been named a finalist for the 2021 Poetry of the Plains & Prairies (POPP) Award.

www.ingramcontent.com/pod-product-compliance
Lightning Source LLC
Chambersburg PA
CBHW030351100526
44592CB00010B/911